ESSENTIAL
MANAGERS

EFFECTIVE
COMMUNICATION

ESSENTIAL MANAGERS
EFFECTIVE
COMMUNICATION

Written by James O'Rourke
Senior Art Editor Gillian Andrews
Project Editor Hugo Wilkinson
US Editors Margaret Parrish, Jill Hamilton
Managing Editor Gareth Jones
Senior Managing Art Editor Lee Griffiths
Production Editor Nikoleta Parasaki
Production Controller Mandy Inness
Jacket Designer Mark Cavanagh
Design Development Manager Sophia M.T.T.
Delhi Team:
Senior Editorial Manager Rohan Sinha
Deputy Managing Art Editor Sudakshina Basu
Produced for Dorling Kindersley Limited
by Cobalt id www.cobaltid.co.uk
Editor Marek Walisiewicz
Designers Paul Reid, Rebecca Johns

First American Edition, 2009
Published in the United States by DK Publishing
345 Hudson Street, New York, New York 10014
A Penguin Random House Company
15 16 17 18 10 9 8 7 6 5 4 3 2 1
001-ND136-May/2015

Published in Great Britain by Dorling Kindersley Limited.

A catalog record for this book is available from the
Library of Congress.

ISBN 978-1-4654-3541-5

DK books are available at special discounts when
purchased in bulk for sales promotions, premiums,
fund-raising, or educational use. For details, contact:
DK Publishing Special Markets, 345 Hudson Street,
New York, New York 10014 or SpecialSales@dk.com.

Color reproduction by Colourscan, Singapore
Printed in China

www.dk.com

Contents

Introduction

Communication is, without question, the most valuable skill any manager can possess. It is the link between ideas and action, the process that generates profit. Communication is the emotional glue that binds humans together in relationships, both personal and professional. The ability to communicate is what connects people to others in an organization, an industry, and a society. To be skilled at it is to be at the heart of what makes enterprise, private or public, function successfully.

Effective Communication focuses on the processes involved in business communication and concentrates, in particular, on ways in which you can become more effective by becoming more knowledgeable and skilled as a communicator. All forms of communication, whether writing, listening, or speaking, are the end products of a process that begins with critical thinking.

This book covers a wide range of topics designed to help you understand the communication process better, from planning a strategy to analyzing your audience. It provides you with guidelines for preparing and delivering an effective speech, as well as ideas for expressing yourself on paper. There are tips for dealing with the specific challenges of team communication, including how to run a meeting, give feedback, and resolve conflict. Finally, it gives you ideas for communicating with clients and customers and thinking about your brand and identity. It's all here. The next step is up to you.

Understanding
communication
skills

Communication is more than just a way to get ideas across or exchange points of view. It is the process by which we interact with others and seek information essential to our daily lives, allowing us to control the circumstances in which we work.

01

Defining communication

Think of communication as a process, involving senders and receivers who encode and decode messages that are transmitted by various media and that may be impeded by noise. The aim of this process is to elicit feedback in order to generate a desired effect or outcome.

Understanding each other

Humans aren't the only beings who communicate—virtually all forms of life are capable of sending and receiving messages. People, however, are the only living organisms known to communicate not just with signals and signs, but through the use of symbols with agreed-upon meanings. If we think about communication as the transfer of meaning, then for each of us, successful communication means

Defining levels of communication

INTRAPERSONAL
Communication **within ourselves**, sending messages to various parts of our bodies, thinking things over, or working silently on a problem.

INTERPERSONAL
Communication **between** or **among people**, sending messages from one person to another—verbally and nonverbally—with the hope of transferring meaning from one person to another.

ORGANIZATIONAL
Communication in the **context of an organization**, sending and receiving messages through various layers of authority and using various channels to discuss topics of interest to the group we belong to or the company we work for.

MASS OR PUBLIC
Sending messages from one person or source to **many people simultaneously**, through television, the internet, or print media.

that you will understand something just as I do: we are in agreement about what the sender intended and what the receiver ultimately understood.

Understanding the principles

Communication involves a number of principles, which apply across time and cultures. The process is always:

- **Dynamic** It is constantly undergoing change.
- **Continuous** Even when you hang up the telephone, you're communicating a message that you have nothing more to say.

- **Circular** Communication is rarely entirely one-way. We each take in information from the outside world, determine what it means, and respond.
- **Unrepeatable** Even if we say something again in precisely the same way, our listeners have heard it before, and so respond to it differently.
- **Irreversible** We cannot "unsay" words: their effect remains even if we're asked to disregard them.
- **Complex** We all assign slightly different meanings to words. This variation is a product of our backgrounds, education, and experience, and means that there is always the potential for misunderstanding.

If communication is the **transfer of meaning**, then for successful communication to occur, you should understand something just as I do

Overcoming barriers

Why do attempts at communication often fail? Broadly speaking, there are two barriers that keep us from communicating successfully: the operations of our bodies and our minds, and our assumptions that other people understand and react to the world in the same way that we do.

Unblocking your communications

The information we receive about the world comes from our senses. It is possible, however, for our senses to be impaired or for the source of the message to provide inadequate information to be reliably decoded. In sending messages to others, we must be sensitive to the fact that they may not see, hear, touch, taste, or smell in the same way we do.

Overcoming barriers to communication

BANISH PREJUDICE

Never make a judgment **before knowing the facts** about a situation. Acknowledge that you are usually working with incomplete data.

CONSIDER CULTURE

Be aware that different **backgrounds, education,** and **experience** give people different expectations. Your way of seeing the world is not the only one.

WATCH YOUR LANGUAGE

Recognize that language has **different levels of meaning**. People will respond differently to the same words, especially if the words are vague or general.

CONTROL YOUR FEELINGS

Try to present your arguments **rationally rather than emotionally**, and accept that other people may have strong feelings about a subject.

FIGHT STEREOTYPES

Don't assume that all members of a group share the same characteristics. **Put aside any stereotypical views** you may have; treat each person as an individual.

In sending messages to others, we **must be sensitive** to the fact that they may not see, hear, touch, taste, or smell **in the same way** that we do

Ensuring understanding

Communication is more than sending and receiving messages; if the message has been delivered but not understood, no communication has taken place. Everything, from the culture in which we live to the norms or standards of the groups to which we belong, can influence how we perceive the messages, events, and experiences of everyday life. Even individual mindsets, such as holding stereotypes, can set up barriers, affecting what we understand and how we react to outside stimuli.

Learn to recognize the barriers likely to block your communications, and focus on what you can do to overcome them. When speaking to someone, for example, constantly monitor their reactions to confirm that you are being fully understood.

Communicating at work

Communication is a skill that is central to the human experience. We each know how to do it; we've done it since birth and receive additional practice each day. So why is it so difficult to communicate on the job? As a manager, it is important to understand how the workplace changes the nature of communication, for both sender and receiver.

Tailoring your approach

Several factors alter the way we look at communication in the business context. We all have a personal communication style, but within an organization you often have to adapt your approach to accommodate the needs of those you work with and work for. If you put the preferences of your audience—particularly your boss and your clients—above your own, you will often get what you want faster. The way you communicate also depends on your position within the organization. The higher your level of responsibility, the more you have to take into account when communicating. And as you become more accountable, you need to keep better records—a form of communication to yourself that may later be read by others.

Adapting to your environment

Organizations, like the people who work in them, are in constant flux. Businesses change by necessity with the conditions of the marketplace and the lives of the managers who run them. Your communications must adapt to the conditions in which you find yourself. However, this never constitutes a reason for signing your name to a document that is false, or passing along information that you know isn't true.

Matching the culture

All communication must work within an organization's culture. The accepted approach can vary considerably between different organizations: some companies, for example, require every issue to be written in memo form and circulated before it can be raised in a team meeting. Other organizations are more "oral" in nature, offering employees the opportunity to talk things through before writing anything down.

Many companies rely on a particular culture to move day-to-day information through the organization. To succeed in such a business, you must adapt to the existing culture rather than try to change it or ask it to adapt to you.

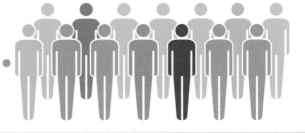

CHECKLIST...
Adapting your style   **YES NO**

1   Do you understand how the **culture of the organization you work for** affects the way in which you need to communicate? ...... ☐ ☐

2   Have you adapted your **writing and speaking style** to meet the expectations of the culture in which you are working? .... ☐ ☐

3   Have you changed your style to accommodate any changes in the **structure of the company** or the conditions of your industry? .... ☐ ☐

4   Have you noted the communication preferences of your supervisor and **adapted** your **writing, speaking, and listening styles** accordingly? .... ☐ ☐

Planning your approach

Getting people to listen to what you say, read what you write, or look at what you show them isn't easy. How do you persuade them that paying attention to your message is in their best interest? The key to ensuring that your communication hits the mark is detailed planning.

Choosing your approach

The choices you make, from the content of the message you send to the medium you select, all have a direct impact on the outcome of your communication. Whatever the situation, ask yourself about the following:

47%

higher returns to shareholders are **reported** in companies that are led by **good communicators**

Tip

QUESTION YOUR OWN ROLE

Ask yourself whether you are the **right person** to send the message. Will your signature compel people to action, or might the message be **more effective** coming from your manager, or someone closer to the intended audience?

Tip

GET TO KNOW YOUR AUDIENCE

It's all too easy to stereotype an audience, especially when you are working against the clock. Make sure you have **collected all the information** available about your audience, and refer to the **key characteristics** as you prepare your speech or document.

Who will receive the message? What is **your relationship** to them? What do they need to know? What **action** do you want them to take?

MESSAGE

What should your message contain? How should your message **impart the information**? Should your message be broad or detailed?

MEDIUM

What's the best way to send this message? Is one medium **quicker** or **cheaper** than another? Will one offer a **better opportunity** for feedback or carry more detail?

CODE

Will your audience understand the words you've used? Will the **words and images** mean the same thing to the audience as they mean to you? Do these words and images have **multiple meanings** for various audiences?

FEEDBACK

How will you know if you've **communicated successfully**? Will the audience response be delayed? Will it be filtered through another source?

NOISE

How many other senders and messages are out there? Whose **message traffic** are you competing with? Will others try to deflect, distort, or disable your communication attempts?

Understanding your audience

Who are these people you're communicating with? What do you know about them? What do they know about you or your subject? How do they feel about it? When preparing to communicate, ask a few simple questions about the people in your audience. Once you know more about them, you can find ways to motivate them to listen.

Considering ethnicity

The ethnic origin of members of your audience may be worth knowing, but don't overestimate its value. The utility of this information may lie in knowing which issues and positions are of greatest concern to members of a particular ethnic group. The limitation lies in knowing that you cannot reasonably stereotype the views of all members of such a group. Sensitivity to ethnic issues and language styles should be sufficient as you prepare a speech.

Audience backgrounds

When you're assessing your audience, look for any similarities in personal backgrounds. For example, what is the average age of audience members? Consider whether they will be familiar with the concepts you plan to speak about, and the sort of life experiences they may have had. Next, think about the education level of your audience. This will have a significant influence on the content of your talk or document, including its central themes and the vocabulary you employ. The personal beliefs of your audience are an important factor to take into account when planning what you will say. Are they liberal or conservative? What is their political affiliation? Are they committed to a particular religious or social point of view?

In focus

GENDER TRAITS

Gender refers to the social and psychological expectations, roles, and views of men and women. Considerable evidence now indicates that this may be among the least useful pieces of information to know about your audience. Why? Because study after study has shown no statistically significant difference in the responses of professional men and women to a wide range of stimuli. Clearly, knowing that your audience might be composed exclusively of one sex or another might alter your approach somewhat, but you would be unwise to assume that you should communicate in one way for men and another for women.

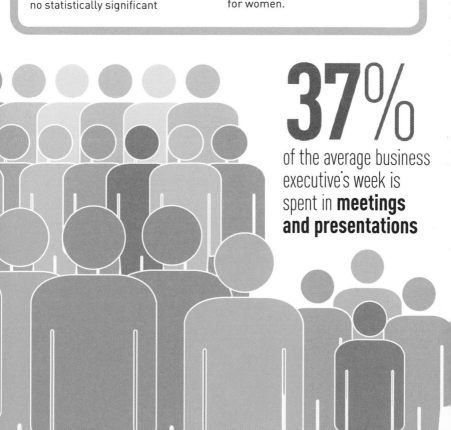

37%

of the average business executive's week is spent in **meetings and presentations**

Socioeconomic factors

For certain forms of communication, knowing the economic status and lifestyle of your audience is especially important. Gain as much information as you can about the following:

- **Occupation** Knowing how people earn their living will tell you something about their educational background and their daily routines, as well as their motivations and interests.

- **Income** Knowing how much money an audience makes can give you some idea of what their concerns are. The less they make, the more they will be driven by basic needs, such as food and housing. American psychologist Abraham Maslow documented the hierarchy of human needs, showing that higher level needs—such as self-actualization—are only relevant to people once their more basic needs have been met.

- **Socioeconomic status** This term describes where your audience is located in the social/economic spectrum. It is, of course, a direct function of other factors, such as income, education, occupation, neighborhood, friends, family, and more. Think of this as a single descriptor that explains just how much prestige your audience has in the eyes of others in their own society, and use it to target your words to address their problems, hopes, and needs.

Targeting your communication

WORK WITHIN OBJECTIVES

All of your communication should be **consistent** with and **directly supportive** of the strategic objectives of your organization—its vision, values, and beliefs.

ADAPT TO YOUR AUDIENCE

Appeal to the **basic needs** (shelter, sustenance, safety, companionship, or social approval) of your intended audience or their **senses** (use motion, color, and sound). What can you do to hold their attention?

EXPLAIN YOUR POSITION

Use words that your audience will **understand** and concepts they can **relate to**. This means, of course, that you must **know who your audience are**, as well as what they know and how they feel about the subject.

MOTIVATE YOUR AUDIENCE

Encourage your audience to accept and act on your message by **appealing to authorities** that they respect, the social conformity displayed by others they **know or admire**, the **rationality** of your argument, or their desire to behave in **consistent ways.**

KEEP THEM ON SIDE

Make your audience resistant to counter-persuasion by asking for a **tangible, preferably public, commitment** from them, or reminding them of the benefits to be derived from doing as you ask.

MANAGE EXPECTATIONS

Always let your audience know **what to expect,** and **deliver what you promise**, never less. People are disappointed only if their expectations exceed what they actually receive.

Matching the message

Once you know something about the individuals who make up your audience, begin to think about how to approach them. You'll need a strategy to help devise the right message and to choose the most effective method of communication for your audience.

Hitting the right knowledge level

A thorough knowledge of what your audience already knows about your subject is useful in a number of ways. First, it tells you where to begin. Don't speak down to the audience by explaining fundamentals they already understand. Second, don't start above their heads. Begin at a point they are comfortable with and move on from there.

Managing emotions

Even more important than what the audience knows about your subject is how they feel about it. What they know about taxation is far less relevant than how they feel about it when they listen to a talk about tax reform. You need to tailor your words carefully to what the emotional response of your audience is likely to be. The greater the degree of ego involvement (or emotional response) to a given topic, the narrower the range

Establishing the audience's role

Your message may need to reach only the audience in front of you, or you may be relying on those people to pass on the message to others. Think about everyone who might see or hear your message, including:

PRIMARY AUDIENCE

These are the people who will receive your written or spoken message directly. Make sure that you **understand and address** their needs, interests, and concerns.

SECONDARY AUDIENCE

Others might read or **hear of your message indirectly**. Could the communication be given to a reporter, union organizer, or competitor?

GETTING YOUR MESSAGE ACROSS

Dos	Don'ts
O **Knowing as much as you can about who will read or hear your words**	O Assuming the audience knows all or nothing about your subject
O **Tailoring your message to the needs and interests of your audience**	O Acting as if the audience already shares your ideas and interests
O **Understanding who the key decision-makers are, and their criteria for making decisions**	O Failing to check who exactly is in your audience, and what they need to know in order to act
O **Knowing who is respected by your audience and seeking their approval for what you recommend**	O Assuming your ideas are good enough to stand up on their own, and not discussing them

of acceptable positions open to you. In other words, people are much more open-minded on topics they are indifferent about than they are on topics they care about passionately. If you misjudge an emotional response, your communication will fail.

Tailor your words carefully to what the **emotional response** of your **audience** is likely to be

GATEKEEPERS

These are the individuals who you have to **route your message** through, and who might filter or block it. Does someone in particular stand between you and the audience you hope to reach?

OPINION LEADERS

These are individuals who have **significant influence** over members of the audience. Who do they admire or listen to on this subject?

KEY DECISION-MAKERS

These are people with the **power to influence** the outcome of the communication.

Choosing your medium

Most managers make decisions about whether to write or speak to someone based on two criteria: convenience and their own personal preferences. But an effective choice of communication medium or channel depends on much more than what suits you at the time.

Learning to ignore instinct

Many managers choose a form of communication instinctively, and not always for the right reasons. For example, if you need to pass bad news to a colleague but don't want to provoke a confrontation, you might choose to send an email, even though your colleague would prefer to hear from you in person. On another occasion, you might choose to make a phone call rather than write a letter, because it seems quicker or easier.

You might make this choice even when the message is complex and would benefit from extensive explanation, detailed description, or visual aids. In fact, just two factors should govern your choice of medium for any message. You should think first about the preferences of the person or audience receiving your message, and second about the characteristics and benefits of speaking versus those of writing.

When to write

Writing produces a **permanent record**, can be used to convey great detail, is often much more precise, and can be used for careful wording. If it's important that you say something in a specific or exact way, you may want to write it down. And, of course, if your audience has a preference for source material or **large amounts of detail**, such as tables or large lists, you can provide that information as an appendix or attachment to a memo, report, or proposal.

Keep in mind that you may have to share your message with many people and it may be impractical or impossible to speak to each of them. Writing in a **precise, persuasive** way may be the best approach to influence your audience.

In focus

THE PLATINUM RULE
We're all familiar with the old rule: "Do unto others as you would have them do unto you." It's a good rule, but it contains a small flaw. What if others don't want to receive the same treatment as you? What if their preferences are, in fact, significantly different? The Platinum Rule, devised by communication expert Tony Alessandra, who has advised companies such as Apple, Ford, and IBM, is a variation of that age-old maxim: "Do unto others as they want to be done unto." This means treat others as they want to be treated, not how you think they should be treated. Communicate with others in the manner that they prefer and you'll get what you want: their time, attention, and cooperation.

When to speak

Speaking provides a **richer context**—it includes the use of nonverbal cues and allows for more emotion. This communication form is **less rigid**, as it leaves no permanent record. It may also be much quicker.

Speaking to others also **invites their participation**. It may be the best way to elicit ideas, size up other people's feelings, and even discover any possible objections to your message before decisions have been made and formalized in writing. Once something is written down, people tend to feel committed to that course of action, even if the documents can easily be revised. A conversation or discussion, on the other hand, has a more transitory feel to it: it is **flowing and flexible**, and less permanent and formal than written forms of communication.

Tip

TURN OFF THE AUTOMATIC PILOT
Don't just choose the easiest form of communication. Stop, consider your options, and choose the right channel and medium for your message.

Speaking
and writing

Two of the most important skills for a manager, and often also the most daunting, are to stand up in front of an audience and deliver a presentation, and to communicate effectively in writing, whether in formal business letters, email correspondence, or detailed reports. For both, clear thinking, preparation, and practice are the keys to success.

02

Planning your speech

Preparing for a business presentation is the most important stage of the process. While it may seem daunting at first, planning your speech becomes much easier once you break the task down into manageable steps, ensuring that you address all the relevant issues at the right time.

Defining substance and style

When it comes to giving a speech, content is king. Substance matters and there is absolutely no substitute for knowing what you're talking about. This means that, whenever possible, you should select a topic that you know and understand, so that you can talk about it with confidence. However, this also depends on your audience; never forget that they are the reason you are in the room. Using your knowledge of your audience to tailor the content to meet their expectations is not a guarantee of success, but it is certainly a step in the right direction.

> Identifying your **role** as a speaker and your **importance** to the listeners is essential

Determining your purpose

Before you start to plan the details of your speech, make sure that you know why you are speaking. If you can't come up with a reason for speaking, then don't speak. Identifying your role as a speaker and your importance to the listeners is especially important. It may be that this audience wants your views on the subject at hand and is keenly interested in your opinions. Alternatively, your purpose may be purely to inform them about a topic, and the demand for your opinions may not be as high as you imagine.

Find out, too, all you can about the context in which the presentation will take place. You need to know the answers to questions such as: is your audience still in the fact-gathering stage, or are they ready to make a decision? What is their reason for listening to you? How urgent is the subject you'll be speaking about? Have recent events, either locally or globally, affected their view of the topic in any way? Are your listeners involved in a process that will require them to take action after hearing what you have to say?

Tip

MAKE TIME FOR RESEARCH

You're being paid for your time preparing and delivering the speech, but the **80:20 rule** applies— spend around 80 percent of your time on **research and preparation**, and only around 20 percent on **practice and delivery**.

CASE STUDY

PREPARING TO SUCCEED

Elizabeth Allen, chief communications officer of the international office supplies firm Staples, Inc., was given the task of drafting a press-conference speech for her CEO, Tom Stemberg, to announce Staples's sponsorship of a new sports arena in Los Angeles. Ms Allen knew that this financial arrangement would be covered by the sports press, not the business press. She also knew that sports figures, civic officials, investors, and reporters would be in the room: "Many people thought the name would be a local, California company.... This was a Boston company putting its name on a Los Angeles landmark. There were cultural factors at work here, as well as political and business factors." As she considered how to prepare the speech, she decided three things: she would reduce her thinking to one or two main points; she would include a few examples and anecdotes that the local audience would relate to; and most importantly, she would cite at least one powerful reason why the relationship between her company and the City of Los Angeles would be productive and long-term.

Preparing your speech

Once you have a clear picture in your mind of why you are giving the presentation, who your audience is, and what they want to hear from you, start to make a detailed plan of your speech. This planning stage is vital, so make sure that you don't leave it to the last minute. You need to be completely familiar with the structure and content of your speech by the time you deliver it. There are eight key steps to preparing a successful presentation.

Steps to preparing a speech

01

COMPOSE A THESIS STATEMENT

Write a **one-sentence declaration** of what you want the audience to **know, understand, believe,** or **do.** Make it brief, simple, comprehensive, and as complete as possible.

02

DEVELOP THE MAIN POINTS

Restrict yourself to just **two or three main points**, so that you will have time to explain and support them all. Make sure that all of your **evidence** relates to and is supportive of your principal reason for speaking.

03

GATHER SUPPORTING MATERIALS

Now gather evidence to support your main points. Use your knowledge of the audience to select the kinds of proof that they will find **most convincing**. Make your evidence **compelling**, **recent**, and fully **transparent** to your listeners.

04

THINK ABOUT STRUCTURE

Consider the order in which you will **deliver the information**, and think about what you will say in your **introduction**, in the **body** of the speech, and in your **conclusion**.

|05

PREPARE YOUR OUTLINE

Write a one-page outline of your speech. Think about the **issues** you plan to raise, the **sequence** in which you will address each of them, and the **evidence** you'll offer your audience in support of those ideas.

You must be **completely familiar** with both the structure and the **content** of your **speech** by the time you **deliver** it

|06

CONSIDER VISUALS

Think about what visuals will best enhance your speech, by helping to **explain**, **reinforce**, and **clarify your main points**. Sometimes it is easier to show the audience something than to say it.

|07

WRITE THE SPEECH

Now prepare the content of your speech in detail. Some people choose to write in **short bullet points**, others write their **script** out more fully. Choose the way that best suits you, but remember that your audience want to hear you **speak to them**, not read to them.

|08

PREPARE YOUR NOTES

Finally, transfer your speech into the **notes you will use to deliver it**. These may be bullet points on a PowerPoint presentation, written notes on notecards, or the full manuscript.

Your purpose may be purely to **inform your audience** about a topic, or to **deliver** your **opinions** and judgments

Developing visual support

Behavioral scientists have known for many years that visual images can have a powerful effect on the process of learning. In some cases, pictures may reach people who simply don't listen well to the spoken word, or who may not understand what the words mean.

How does visual support help?

Behavioral scientists have found that visual support is important in communication for three main reasons:

- It can help explain, reinforce, and clarify the spoken word during a presentation. If you can't say something easily, you may be able to show it to your audience.
- Some people pay more attention to what they see than what they hear, and can more quickly and easily recall information and concepts with a visual component than those that are just spoken aloud.
- People tend to recognize ideas most easily when they are presented as a combination of both words and pictures, rather than when presented as either words or pictures alone.

94%
of **professional speakers**
use PowerPoint or similar software
for part or all of their **presentation**

Choosing when to use it

Displaying information in a visual manner will enhance most presentations, but tends to work best:

O When you have new data for your audience

O When the information you hope to convey is complex or technical in nature

O If your message is coming to the audience in a new context

O For certain types of information—such as numbers, quick facts, quotations, and lists

O For explaining relationships or comparisons

O For revealing geographical or spatial patterns.

Tip

CHOOSE THE RIGHT CHART
Charts and graphs are a useful way to display data. Be sure to select the type of chart (such as a pie chart, bar chart, or line graph) that **most clearly illustrates** any comparisons you want to make, and use color carefully to **emphasize your point**.

Visual support can help **explain**, **reinforce**, and **clarify** the spoken word: try **showing as well as telling**

Using visuals effectively

Good visuals have a number of characteristics in common. The most important is simplicity. The more complex a visual display becomes, the more difficult it is for an audience to understand. Keep your visuals clear, ordered, and simple when trying to explain an important idea or relationship.

Good visuals use color to explain and attract. Very few people tend to have exactly the same taste in colors, but almost everyone appreciates occasions when colors are used meaningfully and consistently. Certain traditions, such as using red numbers or bars to indicate a loss and black ones to indicate profit, allow audiences to quickly grasp information. Try using a simple legend to explain color use on your charts and graphs; it helps the audience and will ensure consistency and simplicity in your visual aids.

> Keep your visuals **clear** and **simple** when trying to explain an **important idea**

Using visuals well

Thinking carefully about the **needs and interests** of your audience as you plan your visual aids

Choosing visuals that **capture the essence** of your main points

Using color in a consistent, careful manner so that related items are **color-coded** and **grouped together**

Making sure your visual support is **simple**, **crisp**, **clean**, and **uncluttered**

Tip

Although you should respect your company's **brand guidelines**, you don't have to be a slave to corporate PowerPoint templates if they result in dull, predictable visuals. Try experimenting with **novel presentation software**, such as Prezi, or make your own slides using your preferred graphics software and save them in a standard format, such as PDF.

40%
increase in the **persuasive effect** of a presentation can be achieved by the careful use of **visual aids**

Limiting the amount of text alongside your visuals to a few key words: this will produce **a more powerful message** than wordy slides

Avoiding generic, or "stock" images, and visuals that are only indirectly related to your main points

Building up a **personal library of images**, symbols, and graphics to enhance your messages

On important occasions, using a **professional graphic designer** to create a polished presentation

Improving your confidence

It's one thing to know your material. It's another matter entirely to believe that you can get up on stage and speak with confidence to a group of strangers. Understanding your message and having a well-organized speech are important to your success, but so is self-confidence.

Improving your delivery

Rehearsal will help improve your speech and raise your level of self-confidence. Simply knowing that you've been through the contents of your speech more than once builds familiarity and is reassuring. It will also ensure you talk for the correct amount of time. A run-through or two will show whether you have too much, too little, or just enough to say. Rehearsal will also help you improve your transitions. By practicing your speech, you'll be able to identify the rough spots and work on smoothing the transition from one point to another and from one part of the speech to another.

Using notes

The best speakers seem to confidently deliver their speeches extemporaneously, or "from the heart," without notes. Such speeches aren't really memorized word-for-word, but rather are thoroughly researched, well rehearsed, and professionally supported. Many extemporaneous speakers will use

their visual support—usually PowerPoint slides—to prompt their memories. Others prefer to work from bullet points on notecards, or use the full manuscript. Whichever you choose, make sure that your notes are simple, easy to follow, and allow you to maintain eye contact with the audience.

Tip

KEEP NOTES SIMPLE

Losing your place in lengthy notes can give your **confidence** a serious knock, so make sure your notes are quick and **easy to use**, giving you the information you need at a glance.

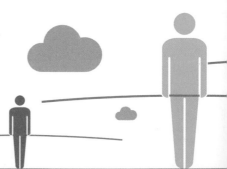

CHECKLIST...
Being prepared   **YES   NO**

1 Have you double-checked the **time and location**
for your speech? .... ☐ ☐

2 Are you sure about the **length of time** allotted to the speech?...... ☐ ☐

3 Have you decided how to **arrange the room**? .... ☐ ☐

4 Have you found out whether you are **using a lectern**
or are free to walk around the room during the speech? .... ☐ ☐

5 Have you tested the **microphone** and **sound system**? .... ☐ ☐

6 Are you familiar with the **arrangements** and **systems**
for visuals? .... ☐ ☐

7 Do you know what **lighting is available,** and have you
determined whether it needs to change for **screen visuals**
or handouts during your talk?.. ☐ ☐

8 If you are **using a computer** during the presentation,
are the relevant files backed up on a second hard drive
to use if necessary? .... ☐ ☐

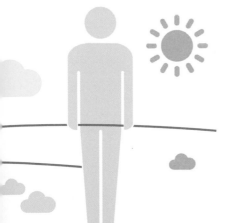

Gaining confidence
The better prepared you are, the more confident you will feel at the podium. Make sure you have thought about all aspects of your presentation, from the layout of the room to the type of microphone you will use. The knowledge that you have personally arranged every detail, and have meticulously planned and rehearsed your talk, will help build your confidence. If you get cold feet, remember that you've been asked to speak because the audience is interested in your expertise and viewpoint. Trust in your ability, intelligence, and confidence to deliver an effective speech.

Delivering your speech

You've researched the topic thoroughly, written and organized your thoughts, and rehearsed your remarks. Use the confidence that you've developed in planning and rehearsal to take the next step: get up and speak. You are the medium, or bearer, of the message, and your delivery is critical to the successful communication of your ideas.

Improving your delivery

As you approach the challenge of becoming an accomplished public speaker, keep in mind that no one is born with great public-speaking ability. Language is the habit of a lifetime, and your ability to speak with conviction and sincerity is a function of your willingness to work at it. Your skills will improve with every speech that you make, and as you master the art of presentation, chances are that others in a position of influence will notice and reward you for your effort.

> Your ability to speak with **conviction** and **sincerity** is a function of your willingness to **work at it**

Ways to keep your audience interested

MAKE A CONNECTION

Step up to the lectern, breathe deeply, smile, think positively, and speak

Humanize and personalize your speech—share your experiences, values, goals, and fears

Do your best to be one of them (unless it's clear you are not)

Use humor where appropriate (unless you are not funny)

Actively involve the audience as much as you can

Focus on current local events and issues known to the audience

HELP THEM UNDERSTAND

Blueprint the speech: tell the audience where your talk is going

Begin with the familiar, then move to the unfamiliar

Talk process first, then add in the detail

Visualize and demonstrate your ideas where you can

Summarize your key points as you progress through a speech

Give examples to illustrate your concepts and ideas

Tell stories, and dramatize your central theme

Use the **confidence** that you've developed in **planning** and **rehearsal** to take the next step: **get up and speak**

Becoming a better writer

Very few people think writing is easy. Good writing—that is, writing with power, grace, dignity, and impact—takes time, careful thought, and revision. Such writing is often the product of many years of training and practice. Even though writing may sometimes seem like hard work, with a little effort you can learn to do it well.

Organizing your writing

Good business writing is simple, clear, and concise. By not calling attention to itself, good writing is "transparent," helping the reader focus on the idea you are trying to communicate rather than on the words that you are using to describe it.

The key to good business writing is organization. You need to know where you are going before you start, so do your research and identify the key issues you need to cover. Compose a list of the most important points, and use them to create an outline. If your document will include an overview section containing your purpose for writing, write this first. Next, tackle the most important paragraphs, before filling out the details and any supplementary material.

Have I "translated" any **technical terms**?

Have I explained adequately?

Does my writing **flow in a logical way**, and have I given **complex explanations** in a step-by-step form?

Use **simple**, **down-to-earth** words, and avoid needless ones and wordy expressions

Writing for clarity

When composing a memo, letter, or report, keep in mind that your reader often doesn't have much time: senior managers, in particular, generally have tight schedules and too much to read. They need your written communication to quickly and clearly give them the details they need to know.

Ensure that your writing style is both precise and concise. Use simple, down-to-earth words, and avoid needless ones and wordy expressions. Simple words and expressions are more quickly understood and can add power to your ideas. Be direct and avoid vague terms such as "very" and "slightly"; this will show that you have confidence in what you are saying and will add power to your ideas. Make sure, too, that everything you write is grammatically correct—you don't want your busy reader to have to reread your sentences to try to decipher their meaning.

Keep your paragraphs short; they are more inviting and more likely to get read. If your document must include numbers, use them with restraint—a paragraph filled with numbers can be difficult to read and follow. Use a few numbers selectively to make your point, then put the rest in tables and graphics.

Have I said enough to **answer questions** and **allay fears** without giving too much detail?

Have I used **visuals** to help explain **complex facts**?

Have I cautioned the reader, where necessary, against **common mistakes** and **misreading** of the information?

80%

of people will read the **headline** of a piece of text; only **20% will read the rest**

Tip

ALWAYS EDIT
Revising and editing are **critical to good writing**. Putting some time between writing and editing will help you be more objective. Revise your writing with the intent to **simplify**, **clarify**, and **trim excess words**.

Making your writing come alive

To escape from outdated, excessively formal writing styles, try to make your writing more like your speaking, and then "tidy it up." Imagine your reader is in front of you and aim all the time for writing that is clear, fresh, and easy to read. You may need to write a first draft for structural purposes, and then go back over your document.

VIGOROUS AND DIRECT

Use **active sentences** and avoid the passive voice. Be **more definite** by limiting the use of the word "not."

Make sure that your writing is:

In focus

THE RIGHT ORDER

A poorly organized letter reads like a mystery story. Clue by clue, it unfolds details that make sense only toward the end—if the reader gets that far. Your job is to make it easier for the reader, by explaining each point with an overview, followed by details. To avoid any confusion, always give directions before reasons, requests before justifications, answers before explanations, conclusions before details, and solutions before problems. Try the approach used in newspaper articles. They start with the most important information and taper off to the least important.

Tip

MAKE IT PERFECT
Eliminate factual errors, typos, misspellings, bad grammar, and incorrect punctuation in your writing. Remember that if **one detail** in a memo you have written is recognized to be incorrect, your entire line of thinking may be considered suspect.

CONNECTING WITH THE READER

Reach out to your reader by occasionally using questions. A request **gains emphasis** when it ends with a question mark. Rather than writing, "Please advise as to whether the meeting is still scheduled for February 21st," simply ask: "Is the meeting still scheduled for February 21st?

MADE UP OF SHORT SENTENCES

This won't guarantee clarity, but short sentences will prevent many of the confusions that can easily occur in longer ones. Try the ear test: **read your writing aloud** and break apart any sentence you can't finish in one breath.

FREE OF CLICHÉS AND JARGON

Tired **words and expressions** make your writing appear superficial.

When **writing** text, imagine that your reader is with you: this will help make your writing **more accessible**

Meeting your reader's needs

Before you write, find out what the reader expects, wants, and needs. If you later discover that you must deviate from these guidelines, let the reader know why. When composing your document, don't include material that you don't need: you may be accused of missing the point. Make sure, too, that you always separate facts from opinions in your writing. The reader should never be in doubt as to what you know to be true, and what you think may be the case. Always apply a consistent approach to avoid misunderstandings.

Capturing and keeping your readers' attention

USE CONTRACTIONS

Make your writing softer and more accessible by occasionally using the contractions that we naturally speak with, such as "I'm," "we're," "you'd," "they've," "can't," "don't," and "let's."

ALLOW SENTENCES TO END WITH A PREPOSITION

Don't reword a sentence just to move a preposition (e.g. "after," "at," "by," "from," "of," "to," or "up") from the end. You are likely to lengthen, tangle, and stiffen the sentence.

WRITE WITH PERSONAL PRONOUNS

Use "we," "us," and "our" when speaking for the company. Use "I," "me," and "my" when speaking for yourself. Either way, be generous with the use of the word "you."

USE THE PRESENT TENSE WHENEVER POSSIBLE

This adds immediacy to your writing. Be careful, however, not to slip from the present to the past tense and back again, because this will make your writing confusing. Select one tense and stick to it.

Find out what your reader **expects**, **wants**, and **needs**: if you deviate from this in your writing, **let the reader know why**

USE SHORT TRANSITIONS

Use "but" more than "however," and "more than" rather than "in addition to." Use more formal transitions only for variety. Don't be afraid to start a sentence with words like "but," "so," "yet," "and," or "or."

Writing a business letter

Business letters are primarily external documents, although managers will occasionally use letters to correspond with subordinates and executives within their organization. Good letters are crisp, concise, and organized so that readers can follow and understand the content with little effort.

Writing successful letters

Your success as a business writer depends, in large measure, on your ability to convince others that what you have written is worth their attention. This is more likely if your letter meets three criteria: it should be concise, it should be informal, and it absolutely must be organized. Be careful, however. Brevity is desirable, but you can overdo it. Make sure that your letters are not too brief or curt. It is extremely important to make sure that your reader has enough information to understand the subject. Include each issue relevant to the subject, and explain the process, the outcome, or the decision to the satisfaction of the reader. If you were receiving the letter, would the information be sufficient? Would you be satisfied that the writer had taken you seriously?

Tip

BE PROMPT
When you receive a business letter, always **send an answer within three business days**. If you can't reply within this time—because you need to speak with someone else or gather information—drop the writer a note to **let them know** that you are working on their problem.

Showing interest

When responding to a letter you have received, aim to show that you are genuinely interested. The person writing to you thought the issue was important enough to write about; you should think so, too. Show by your words and actions that you care about the person and the contents of the letter.

Give everyone the benefit of the doubt. Don't automatically assume that the person corresponding with you is doing so for the purpose of cheating you or your company.

Hitting the right tone

If a correspondent makes a joke, play along. Show that you have a sense of humor; however, consider the culture of your audience and keep in mind that some humor may not translate well.

If you have to deliver bad news by letter, say you are sorry. Use phrases such as, "I am sorry to say that..." or "I regret to say that we'll be unable to [do something] because..." You can soften the blow by saying that you're sorry it happened, or that you regret the outcome. If it's bad news and your reader thinks you don't care, you may spark an unwanted reaction. If you're bearing good news, say that you are glad: "I am delighted to tell you that..." Alternatively use a phrase such as: "You will be pleased to learn that..."

Keep a cool head

Never write and quickly send off an angry letter. Venting your spleen in an angry, hostile reply to someone may make you feel good, but it's almost never a good idea to post such a letter. Take your time and cool down before you compose an angry letter. Then, if you have written something you aren't sure about, wait until the following day so that you can reread it before sending. Chances are, you'll think twice about mailing.

A letter should be **informal** and **organized**. Brevity is desirable, but you can overdo it: make absolutely sure that your reader has enough information to **understand the subject**

In focus

FORM LETTERS

It may be tempting to compile a "one-size-fits-all" approach to writing when there are many recipients, but it is usually a recipe for disaster. A letter must answer all of the questions its audience is likely to have, responding to their fears, doubts, and concerns. In situations in which it is absolutely necessary to use this approach, you can test market form letters, by showing them to several people who are (or have been) members of the audience in question and asking for suggestions for improvement.

Using email and texts effectively

Email is now a key means of staying in touch, passing data and graphics, and managing the flow of information needed to run a business. Text, or SMS, messaging, when properly managed, can also be become a productivity booster, a direct, interactive link to customers, and an essential tool to communicate with other staff.

Reducing your emailing time

Email is a tool; don't let it become your master. Limit the time you spend on email by following these tips:

- **Send less, get less** Think carefully about whether you really need to draft new messages or respond to those you've already received.
- **Escape the endless reply loop** Silence in response to an email message may feel rude, but is acceptable. If you wish to reassure someone that no reply is necessary, finish a message with "no reply needed," or a request with "Thanks in advance." Avoid asking any questions for which you don't really want or need answers.
- **Think twice about the "cc" box** If you copy in a large number of people to your emails and they all respond with a reply that needs an answer, you may create unnecessary traffic.

Sending better emails

Pick the subject line of the email carefully: make it informative and brief so the recipient can easily find and act on it.

1

Be careful with criticism: be sure to provide enough context and background to avoid a misunderstanding.

4

Keep it short. If you need more than three paragraphs, call instead or send the material as an attachment.

5

CHECKLIST...
Knowing when email is not appropriate | **YES** | **NO**

1 Do I need to **convey or discern emotion**? ☐ ☐
2 Do I need to **cut through** the communication clutter? ☐ ☐
3 Do I need to **move quickly**? ☐ ☐
4 Do I want a remote communication **to be private**? ☐ ☐
5 Am I trying to **reach someone** who doesn't have (or check) email? ☐ ☐
6 Do I want to **engage people** and get an **immediate response**? ☐ ☐

> Be sparing in your use of email: think very carefully about whether you really need to **draft new messages** or respond to those you've **already received**

2
Now **write the main body** of the email, using correct grammar, punctuation, and capitalization.

3
Avoid abbreviations and cyberjargon: most business professionals dislike them. WIDLTO (when in doubt, leave them out).

6
Use a signature to conclude your email, but keep it simple: don't be tempted to add humorous or "inspiring" quotes.

7
Before you send the email, **check your attachments.** Send only those that your recipient needs or wants to see.

Developing good email habits

Don't check your email constantly. Check it at regular intervals, such as first thing in the morning, once after lunch, and again before going home. Be disciplined about your email management. Aim to handle each message just once. If it's unimportant or irrelevant, hit the delete key. If you spend more than three hours a week sorting through junk mail, you have a problem and need to reorganize your system.

If a message is something you'll need to respond to, decide whether to do it now or later, when you will have the time and information you need. Once you have responded, move the message out of your inbox and into an archive folder.

An inexpensive way to reach out to customers

High open rates: more than 90 percent of texts are opened and read by recipients

Advantages of text communication

Tip

ESTABLISH A RESPONSE TIME

If you usually respond to email messages immediately, people grow to **expect an immediate response**, and become annoyed if you differ from this. The rule of thumb in business is to respond to emails by the **end of the same day**. If it's really urgent, use the telephone instead.

Concise—your message must be less than 160 characters in length, so is more likely to be read and absorbed

Texts have their place in a **work environment**, as long as you define what they should and should not be used for

Almost instant delivery

Environmentally friendly—creates no paper waste

Texts as a business tool

Using text messages to reach out to customers is established practice in many businesses, but relatively few companies use texts for other types of business communications. The reason for this is that the content of a text message can be perceived as being trivial, impermanent, and not tied to any coherent communications strategy. However, texts do have their place in a work environment, as long as you define what they should—and should not—be used for. Texts are an ideal medium for alerts, such as notifications of downtime of computer servers; they can be used for company announcements, to motivate staff, or to quickly introduce new members of a team to the company. Avoid using texts to explain complex ideas, or when you need a verifiable information trail.

Writing reports

Reports are longer and more comprehensive than most documents, and are written for the purpose of documenting actions, describing projects and events, and capturing information on complex issues. They are often written by more than one person for audiences with multiple needs and interests.

Planning your report

There are three main questions to consider when compiling a report:

- **Who is in your audience?** Think about their level of interest in the content, and their familiarity with the issues, ideas, and vocabulary you plan to use.
- **What is the ideal format?** Consider how your readers will use the document—will they start from the beginning and read through page by page, or will they skip to sections that interest them most?
- **Is the document properly organized?** Consider using a bold typeface for headings and subheadings to help organize the information and make it retrievable.

Busy business leaders may only read the **executive summary** of a report, so it must tell them all they need to know in order for them to **understand** your recommendations

Tip

INCLUDE A COVER LETTER

As a courtesy to your reader, always include a cover letter to accompany the report, explaining **what the report covers and why**. Where appropriate, include the report's most **important recommendations** or **findings**.

Writing the report

Reports are divided into three sections: front matter (including title page, abstract, table of contents, and list of figures and tables), the main body of the report, and end matter (bibliography, appendices, glossary, and index). Begin the main body with an executive summary, detailing the report's key points and recommendations. Busy executives may only read this section, so it must tell them all they need to know in order for them to agree with your recommendations.

Dividing your report into sections

SECTION	CONTENT
TITLE PAGE	A single page containing the full title of the report, the names of the authors, the date of issue, and the name of the organization to which the report is submitted.
ABSTRACT	A paragraph that summarizes the major points. It enables a reader to decide whether to read the entire work.
TABLE OF CONTENTS	A list of all of the headings within the report in the order of their appearance, along with a page number for each.
LIST OF FIGURES AND TABLES	Reports with more than five figures or tables should include a page listing each one with its page number.
FOREWORD (OPTIONAL)	An introductory statement usually written by an authority figure. It provides background information and places the report in the context of other works in the field.
PREFACE (OPTIONAL)	This describes the purpose, background, or scope of the report.
EXECUTIVE SUMMARY	This provides more information than the abstract, and enables readers to scan the report's primary points. These summaries are usually restricted to a few pages.
MAIN TEXT	This forms the main body of the report, and explains your work and its findings.
CONCLUSION	This contains not only concluding remarks but also any recommended actions for the readers.
BIBLIOGRAPHY	A listing of all the sources consulted to prepare the report; it may also suggest additional reading and resources.
APPENDICES	Information that supplements the main report as evidence, such as lists, tables of figures, and charts and graphs.
GLOSSARY	An alphabetical list of definitions of unusual terms used.
INDEX	An alphabetical list of topics with page numbers.

Communicating
with your team

A team is only as good as its communication; misunderstandings can cause a huge amount of extra work and lost time. When managing a team, focus on giving constructive feedback, briefing thoroughly, and dealing effectively with conflict.

03

Listening effectively

Studies show that adults now spend more than half of their daily communication time listening to someone else speak. As a manager, being able to listen effectively and understand others is at the heart of creating a team that performs to the best of its ability.

Learning when to listen

Listening is a skill you acquire naturally, but can improve upon if you're motivated to do so. The first step toward becoming a better listener is, surprisingly, to stop: you need to stop talking, stop trying to carry on more than one conversation, and stop interrupting. Let the other person speak. As others are talking, allow yourself to respond cognitively and emotionally, taking in the factual information and the tone of their remarks, without responding. Then ask carefully thought-out questions that will clarify what they have said and reassure you of its basis in fact.

Tip

BEWARE WISHFUL THINKING
Just because you want to hear something doesn't mean it is what the speaker is **actually saying**. It is all too easy to fall into the trap of **selective hearing**, so make sure that you listen to everything that the speaker is telling you.

75%

of what you say to others is not **absorbed** or remembered by them. How can you be sure that they are **receiving** the **most important** parts of your message?

Getting the message

Start by trying to see things from the speaker's point of view, and let your actions demonstrate this. Show interest with your body language: look the speaker in the eyes and maintain an open and nonthreatening posture. Give the speaker physical signs of your undivided attention: close the door, hold your calls, and put aside whatever you're working on.

Listen carefully to how something is said: look out for hints of sarcasm, cynicism, or irony in what you hear. Try to tune in to the speaker's mood and intention. Communication is a shared responsibility, so it is up to you to ensure that you understand the message.

Once you have listened to what a person has to say and clarified anything you're not sure of, evaluate the facts and evidence. Ask yourself whether the evidence is recent, reliable, accurate, and relevant.

To become a better listener, you need **stop talking**, stop trying to carry on more than one conversation, and **stop interrupting** and let the other person speak

LISTENING ACTIVELY

Dos	Don'ts
O Listening regularly to difficult material to hone your listening ability	O Assuming that everything interesting should be provided in written form
O Giving your full and undivided attention to the speaker	O Pretending to listen while actually doing something else
O Listening to the argument in the speaker's terms, and in the order he or she wishes to follow	O Criticizing the speaker's delivery and interrupting the flow of what they are saying to ask questions
O Focusing on the reasons for the speaker's approach and discussion	O Assuming you already know what the issue is and how to resolve it

Giving feedback

When he was mayor of New York City, Ed Koch frequently walked the streets of his hometown asking his constituents, "How am I doing?" The question wasn't simply rhetorical. He asked the question of friend and foe alike, and he cared about the responses, because his performance as mayor depended on feedback—direct, honest, current, unfiltered feedback.

When to give feedback

Good feedback doesn't just happen. It is the product of careful, deliberate communication strategies, coupled with good interpersonal communication skills. You can significantly increase the probability that the feedback you give helps others improve by understanding the role of feedback in both personal and professional settings.

Feedback is vital to any organization committed to improving itself, because it is the only way for managers to know what needs to be improved. Giving and receiving feedback should be more than just a part of an employee's behavior; it should be a part of the whole organization's culture.

How to give feedback

Providing constructive, useful feedback involves more than simply responding to people as they speak to you. Consider the context in which the communication takes place, people's intentions as they speak (or choose not to speak), and your objectives as a manager.

GIVE BOTH POSITIVE AND NEGATIVE FEEDBACK

People are more likely to **pay attention** to your complaints if they have also **received your compliments.** It is important to remember to tell people when they have done something well.

Tip

FOCUS ON BEHAVIOR

If you are giving negative feedback, defuse any hostility and **minimize the fear** felt by the other person by depersonalizing the conversation: focus your comments on the behavior involved, not the people.

Giving and receiving feedback should be a part of the whole organization's culture

In focus

LANGUAGE

Not everyone has the same understanding of language, and certain words, phrases, or terms that mean one thing to a manager may mean something very different to a person receiving feedback. It is important, therefore, that the language used for feedback is acceptable to the person being spoken to and appropriate for the circumstances. The words used must be clearly understood and agreed upon by both parties. Acronyms or company jargon are only acceptable if it is clear that both parties know what they mean. Successful managers make sure they know whether the person they are giving feedback to shares the same frame of reference they do, avoid language that will cause confusion, and choose words that are universally understood.

GET THE TIMING RIGHT

Before deciding to offer feedback, decide whether the **moment is right** for both people involved. Constructive feedback can happen only within a **context of listening to** and **caring about** the other person. If the time isn't right, if the moment isn't appropriate, you can always delay briefly before offering your thoughts.

UNDERSTAND THE CONTEXT

This is the most important characteristic of feedback: find out where an event happened, why it happened, and what led up to it. Always **review the actions** and decisions that led up to the moment; never simply give feedback and leave.

Understanding nonverbal communication

Most of the meaning transferred from one person to another in a personal conversation comes not from the words that are spoken, but from nonverbal signals. Learning to read, understand, and use these wordless messages isn't easy, but is essential for effective communication

Reading nonverbal signals

The movement, positioning, and use of the human body in various communication settings serves a number of functions:

- To highlight or emphasize some part of a verbal message
- To regulate the flow, pace, and back-and-forth nature of verbal messages
- To reinforce the general tone or attitude of a message
- To repeat what the verbal messages convey (holding up three fingers to indicate the number three, for example)
- To substitute for, or take the place of, verbal messages (such as giving a "thumbs up" gesture).

Nonverbal cues are often difficult to read, especially because there are few body movements or gestures that have universally agreed-upon meanings. A colleague who looks tired or overworked to one person may appear disinterested or

> Body language can contradict the **verbal messages** being sent

Using nonverbal signals

indifferent to another. While looking for meaning in a particular movement, position, or gesture, be careful not to miss more important signals that reveal the true feelings of a speaker. Body language can sometimes contradict the verbal messages being sent. Tears in a person's eyes, for example, might involuntarily contradict a message telling you that the speaker is fine.

55%

of a message may be conveyed by **facial expression**, according to some psychological studies

WATCH YOUR APPEARANCE
Make sure that your clothing and grooming are appropriate to your audience, your reasons for communicating, and the occasion.

RESTRAIN YOUR MOVEMENTS
Small gestures, close to your body, will convey an image of confidence and authority. Keep your voice low but audible and your posture relaxed.

TAKE CARE WITH TOUCH
The rules on touching others in a business context vary from culture to culture. Make sure you know and respect local customs.

WATCH YOUR EYE CONTACT
Eye contact usually reinforces trust; however, in some Asian cultures, looking a superior in the eye as you speak can be considered disrespectful.

USE VOCAL DYNAMICS
Tone, volume, rate, pitch, forcefulness, and enunciation all convey meaning about a subject, and how you feel about the people in the room.

Running briefings and meetings

Briefings and meetings are an inescapable part of business life. They are a means of sharing information, initiating strategies, perpetuating a culture, and building consensus around business goals. Done well, they're good for business and good for morale.

Organizing a meeting

Be clear about the purpose of any meeting before you start planning. Invite only those people who are directly related to your goals, and make sure you include all the key decision-makers. Once you've arranged a time, place, and date that is convenient to everyone, send them all an agenda, making clear the meeting's theme and goals. In putting together the agenda, consider the following questions: What do we need to do in this meeting? What conversations will be important to those who attend? What information will we need to begin?

Prioritize the most important items so they will be discussed early on in the meeting, and assign a certain amount of time for each agenda item.

Giving a briefing

Briefing is a process by which you provide information to those who need it. As with any form of communication, think about your audience, your purpose, and the occasion. Find out all you can about the audience, and what they hope to take away from the session. State your purpose clearly and simply at the beginning of the meeting: "The purpose

ASK YOURSELF...
Do I need to call a meeting?

		YES	NO
1	Do I need to **motivate people**, giving them a jump-start to get going?	☐	☐
2	Do I need to **share** general company or market **information** with people to help them do their jobs?	☐	☐
3	Do I need to **initiate a new program** or project?	☐	☐
4	Do I wish to **introduce people** to one another, so they can benefit from each other's experiences?	☐	☐

CASE STUDY

A COMPETITIVE ADVANTAGE

As CEO of the international retail giant Walmart, David Glass knew the company would have to be quick off the mark with merchandising strategies, particularly in response to moves made by competitors. Each Saturday morning, when sales results for the week were transmitted to the corporate headquarters, Glass would gather key subordinates to share information from people in the field. They would tell the sales team what their competitors were doing; the senior team would then focus on corrective actions they wanted to take. By noon, regional managers would telephone district managers, and they would discuss and agree the changes they would implement in the next week. "By noon on Saturday," Glass said, "we had all our corrections in place. Our competitors, for the most part, got their sales results on Monday for the week prior. They were already 10 days behind."

of this briefing is to look at budget projections for the next 90 days." Let them know why you're calling the meeting now.

Delivering a brief

When giving a briefing meeting, choose the delivery that best suits your speaking style and the needs of the audience. There are three forms to choose from:

- **Memorized presentations** These are delivered verbatim, just as you wrote them. This gives you total control over the material, but unless you're a trained actor, there's a risk that you'll sound wooden and the material contrived. Worse yet, you may forget where you are and have to start again or refer to notes.
- **Scripted briefings** These are more common, but they can also sound stilted. The problem with reading is that you risk losing eye contact, lowering your chin, and compressing your vocal pitch. If you do use a script, rehearse carefully and look up frequently, making regular eye contact with your audience.
- **Extemporaneous briefings** These are delivered either without notes or with visual aids to prompt your memory. They are the most effective choice, looking more spontaneous, while actually being thoroughly researched, tightly organized, and well rehearsed.

Tip

ANTICIPATE QUESTIONS

Do your best to **address** audience concerns, questions, doubts, and fears in advance. **Plan the content** of your briefing around the needs of those in the audience

Communicating to persuade

Whether your are trying to sell a product, convince your superiors to release more resources, convince an investor, or win a promotion, you need a clear strategy to persuade your audience. Removing the barriers to people saying "yes" is a two-way process.

Understanding the audience

Before you can expect your request to be understood and considered, you first need to understand your audience. What are their interests, their motivators, and their possible objections to your proposal? Most successful attempts at persuasion involve four separate, yet related, steps. Following these steps won't guarantee success with any particular audience, but they will set the stage for the attitudes you're trying to shape in your team and the behavior you hope will follow.

GETTING THEIR ATTENTION

If you want to motivate people to do something, you first have to catch their attention. Research shows that we **selectively choose** what to pay attention to, both as a defense mechanism against sensory overload, and because we **seek out messages with particular value** for us. We ignore virtually everything else. There are two ways to capture attention:

- Use **physical stimuli**, such as bright lights, sound, motion, or color.
- Present stimuli that **relate directly to the needs** or goals of those you want to persuade.

PROVIDING A MOTIVATION

Next, you need to **provide a reason** for people to act. A persuasive writer or speaker is one who can **lead others to believe in** what he or she is advocating, and then encourage some form of behavior in line with that belief. This amounts to giving good reasons for what you believe. These are not reasons you think are good, but reasons your team thinks are good.

Identify the needs and interests of your team and connect them to your message. Which of their needs are you fulfilling? **Appeal to their sense of rationality**—show why it makes sense to act on your message. Or **call on their sense of conformity**, by showing how well others will view them if they act on your message.

When to use one- or two-sided arguments

ONE-SIDED ARGUMENT	TWO-SIDED ARGUMENT
The audience initially agrees with you and your aim is simply to intensify support.	You suspect or know that the audience initially disagrees with your position.
The audience will not be exposed to any form of counter-persuasion.	You know the audience will be exposed to subsequent counter-persuasion
The audience is not well educated or may become easily confused by an opponent's argument or evidence.	You hope to produce a more enduring result with a knowledgeable audience.

MOVING OTHERS TO ACT

Once you have captured the attention of those you want to persuade and have given them good cause to believe the message, you must provide them with a **clear channel for action**.

First, however, take time to **reassure** them: show them that there is a high probability that **you can deliver** on the promised reward. Your team needs to know that what you've promised will actually come true.

Next, **recommend a specific proposal for action**. Tell your team exactly what you want them to do, describe how you would like them to go about it, and set out a realistic timescale. Make sure that everyone on your team knows how and when **progress will be measured** and identify the end point and the rewards for achievement that lie ahead.

KEEPING THEM ON SIDE

The arguments that you use to persuade others can be one-sided, presenting your case alone, or two-sided, presenting your case as well as dealing with real and potential counterarguments. **Choose your approach** based on the knowledge and preconceptions of your audience. If you decide to use a two-sided argument, you should:

- Warn your team that others may try to change their minds.
- **State some opposing arguments** and then refute them. If you are aware of an opposing message, consider previewing at least part of it to the audience and then explaining why it is flawed.
- **Encourage commitment** in some tangible or visible way. It's more difficult for people to back away from positions for which they've publicly proclaimed their support.

Managing conflict

Conflict can arise from a variety of sources, but many experts see it as a function of such workplace issues as personality, personal and professional relationships, cultural differences, working environments, demands of the marketplace, and of course, competition. As organizations increasingly use teamwork, differences among team members can lead to conflict.

LIMITED RESOURCES

Everything from office space to budgets may put people in competition with one another. Allocate scarce resources fairly to avoid this.

VALUES, GOALS, AND PRIORITIES

Confrontation can occur when people in an organization don't agree on strategic direction or basic priorities. Agreement on goals, large and small, can help to avoid this.

Identifying the sources of conflict

Not all conflict within an organization is unhealthy, but conflict between and among people within an organization can quickly become counter-productive, divisive, and destructive if not properly managed. Conflict may develop over any number of issues or factors, but these five appear regularly:

HUMAN DRIVE FOR SUCCESS

Conflicts can arise as a result of the natural sense of goal orientation that every human experiences. Many organizations actively foster a sense of competition among their members, creating many competitors and few rewards.

CHANGE

Many changes, including those to annual budgets, organizational priorities, lines of authority, or limits of responsibility, as well as restructuring, mergers, divestitures, and layoffs, can create anxiety, uncertainty, and conflict in an organization.

POORLY DEFINED RESPONSIBILITIES

Conflict may result from differences between formal position descriptions and daily expectations of the job. Review and agree who is responsible for what (and to whom).

Conflict resolution techniques

Resolving conflicts between team members is an important function of an effective manager. To begin the process, you should first ensure that both parties acknowledge that the conflict exists and the effects that it is having on team performance and morale. It may be that one party sees the problem as trivial, or is ignoring the issue. Next, encourage the parties to set aside time to address the problem—schedule the first meeting, and offer to participate in the process.

Get people to **agree on the small stuff** first: when this happens, the big issues become **easier to address**

LISTEN CAREFULLY
Find out what's on people's minds, and ask them what they're thinking and how they feel

FOCUS ON INTERESTS
Don't focus on a person's demands, but on their interests—the reasons behind their demands.

RECOGNIZE FEELINGS
Accept feelings in others, and work to communicate empathy. Keep your own emotions in check, to ensure that you act professionally.

SEPARATE PEOPLE FROM PROBLEMS
Rather than saying "I can't support you," say "I'm not in favor of that solution."

KEEP COMMUNICATING

Keep the lines of communication open and speak as frankly and honestly as possible.

START SMALL

Get people to agree on the small stuff first. Once they start to agree on a few things, the big issues won't be as difficult.

Reconciling two sides

SUMMARIZE THE AGREEMENT

Review all the details with everyone involved. Make sure all are in agreement.

DEVISE OPTIONS

Find alternatives for mutual gain. By working together on the options, you can shift the dynamic from competition to cooperation.

CUT YOUR LOSSES

Sometimes the conflict has simply gone too far, and you must decide to make personnel changes.

FIND THE SOURCE

Track the conflict to its source. Don't accept the first answers you find; employees may have underlying concerns.

Communicating
externally

In today's global economy, you may find yourself communicating across companies, countries, and cultures, through a variety of media, including the internet. Focus on your company's core goals and identity to ensure consistent messaging.

04

Negotiating successfully

Negotiation is a process in which people attempt to persuade others to cooperate or assist in attaining goals or goods that they value. The process often involves bargaining—giving up something in order to get something else—as well as collaboration, cooperation, and compromise.

Exploring interests

A key distinction to make in negotiating is recognizing the difference between interests and positions. A position is a hard line in the sand: a statement of a single acceptable outcome. Interests, on the other hand, are the reasons behind that position. Spend time seeing the negotiation from the other party's point of view; this may help you anticipate what is really important to them. This is important because there may be more than one way of meeting those interests. Can you find an alternative, workable position that will still satisfy the other party's interests?

> Don't make a big **concession** right away—the other side may think there is a lot of **"give" in your position**

Making the opening offer

If you have done your homework and have a good idea of the bargaining range, then you should make the opening offer. That offer anchors the bargaining process. Your opening offer should reflect your aspirations, but not be ridiculous. If it is way out of range, you risk insulting the other party and damaging trust. If the other party makes the opening offer, and it is outrageous, don't discuss it. Simply dismiss it, indicate that it is not a possibility, and start again.

Your opening offer should leave you room to make concessions, but bear in mind that any you do make will provide the other party with information. If they make concessions, you should reciprocate, or they may view you with distrust and become more competitive. Don't make too large a concession right away, however, or the other side may think there is considerable "give" in your bargaining range.

Tip

CONSIDER COMPENSATION

Sometimes parties can be **enticed into an agreement** through the offer of something unrelated to the issues in negotiation. Think about **what might be valuable** to the other party, but inexpensive for you to offer.

Recognizing significant points

YOUR TARGET OR ASPIRATION POINT

What you hope to achieve. Set this at a high but reasonable level.

YOUR BEST ALTERNATIVE TO A NEGOTIATED AGREEMENT (BATNA)

This is your back-up plan in case you are unable to reach agreement with the other party.

YOUR RESERVATION OR WALK-AWAY POINT

The least desirable outcome that you will accept. At anything less than your reservation, you would be better off walking away without a deal.

ASK YOURSELF...
Am I prepared to negotiate?

	YES	NO
1 Do I know what I **really want**?	☐	☐
2 Do I know what the **other party** really wants?	☐	☐
3 Should I **cooperate** with them?	☐	☐
4 Should I **reveal** all that I know?	☐	☐
5 Should I **trust** the people I'm negotiating with?	☐	☐

Selling

Selling is both a form of persuasion and a process of relationship building. Most people don't want to feel as if they're being sold something; they would prefer to believe that they're buying it. This involves a balance of thoughtful questions, active listening, and a well-prepared presentation.

Prospecting and presenting

Selling involves actively looking for prospects who have the money, the authority, and a desire to buy. Before you contact a prospect, make sure that they fulfill these criteria, and that you know both what you want to achieve, and how. Develop a presentation that you can deliver confidently. This may be entirely memorized, formulaic (allowing some buyer–seller interaction), or entirely flexible and interactive.

If you're offering a solution to a specific problem, base your proposal around a detailed analysis of the buyer's situation. Before you contact a prospect, always:

- Determine your call objectives. Are they specific, measurable, achievable, realistic, and well-timed?
- Develop a customer profile. What do you know about the person who is making the buying decision?
- Familiarize yourself with all the customer benefits.
- Develop a sales presentation.

Closing the sale

First ask the prospect's opinion about the benefits you're offering, using a question such as: "How does this sound to you?" If this throws up any objections, handle them as they arise. Don't repeat negative statements or concerns; focus on positive outcomes. There are various ways to close a sale, so choose the one that is most appropriate to your situation.

Ways to close a sale

USE THE MINOR POINTS CLOSE

Ask the prospect to make low-risk decisions on minor, low-cost elements. Then ask for the order.

Develop a presentation that you can deliver **confidently**. It may be **memorized**, **formulaic**, or entirely flexible and **interactive**

Tip

MAKE A POSITIVE FIRST IMPRESSION

Be positive: smile, be enthusiastic, and open conversation with a **thoughtful compliment** or a **prediction** related to your product.

USE THE ASSUMPTIVE CLOSE

When the prospect is **close to a decision**, say: "I'll call your order in tonight."

GIVE AN ALTERNATIVE CHOICE

Give **two options**, and then ask: "Which of these do you prefer?"

SUMMARIZE THE BENEFITS

Present the main **features**, **advantages**, and **benefits**, then ask for the order.

USE THE SCARCITY CLOSE

If true, tell the prospect that these items are **so popular**, there may not be many of them left.

USE THE CONTINUOUS "YES" CLOSE

Develop a **set of questions** the prospect will answer "yes" to, then ask for the order.

Communicating across countries and cultures

The industrialized nations of the world are experiencing unprecedented change. In much of Europe, for example, it is possible for EU citizens to travel from country to country without a passport, conducting transactions in a common currency. Barriers to trade have tumbled or vanished in recent years, but through it all, each of us has retained something essential to our identity as humans: our culture.

Defining culture

Culture is everything that people have, think, and do as members of their society. Culture affects and is a central part of our economy and the organizations that employ us. It is composed of material objects, ideas, values, and attitudes, as well as expected patterns of behavior. Whatever your business, you're likely to encounter people of different ethnicity, citizenship, and cultural origin. Dealing with people of different cultures, conducting business over international borders, traveling safely, and communicating effectively are not always easy, but are essential for success in today's business world.

> Culture is composed of material **objects**, **ideas**, **values**, and **attitudes**

Understanding culture

When you're communicating with a culture other than your own, you need to **be sensitive** about the particular beliefs and values of that culture, and how they differ from your own.

CULTURE IS INGRAINED

Few of us would give a moment's thought to learning how to be a part of the culture we have grown up in. Our first culture is so **closely defined** for each of us that we're barely aware that we have one. Learning a second culture, though, takes a **purposeful effort**.

Recognizing change

The culture of any country is constantly undergoing change. The clothing people wear, the transportation they use, the books they read, the topics they talk about, and so on, all change over time. This is due to the internal forces of discovery, invention, and innovation; and external forces, including the diffusion of ideas from other cultures. Some cultures change fast, while others evolve more slowly, either by preference or because they are more physically isolated. Changes in culture are often reflected in changes in the way people speak and write; make sure that your own communications reflect these changes.

Tip

INVESTIGATE THE SUBCULTURES

Virtually all large, complex cultures contain subcultures. These are small groups of people with **separate** and **specialized interests** —essentially, they are niche markets.

CULTURE IS UNIVERSAL

All societies have an interest in passing along values and norms to their children, thereby creating and **defining a culture**. No matter where you travel, you'll find people with cultures that differ from the one in which you grew up; noticing these differences will **strengthen your communications**.

CULTURES ALLOCATE VALUES

Some cultures **engage in behaviors** that others might consider reprehensible. Be careful never to cause offense when communicating by inadvertently breaking taboos or talking about matters that are considered "off limits."

Communicating internationally

On a personal level, communicating across international borders means becoming more aware of the ways in which your thinking or actions are culturally biased.

Start by recognizing that your own education, background, and beliefs may be considered fine, or even laudable in your own culture, but they may not count for so much to someone from a different country. Take a nonjudgmental position toward those from other cultures, and you are likely to find that they will extend the same hospitable tolerance toward you. If you find yourself making personal judgments, keep them to yourself. When you're writing or speaking to people from another culture, try to understand life

Tip

LEARN TO RECOGNIZE "NO"

Some cultures consider it rude to say "no." If you are met with vague answers to requests, such as **"I'll try"** or **"yes, but it may be difficult"** in these cultures, it may be safer to assume that your request has been refused.

from their perspective. Learn to communicate respect for other people's ways, their country, and their values.

In focus

ETHNOCENTRISM

All cultures, to one degree or another, display ethnocentrism: the tendency to evaluate a foreigner's behavior by the standards of one's own culture, and to believe that one's culture is superior to all others. We tend to take our own culture for granted. We're born into it, and we live with its rules and assumptions day in and day out. We quickly come to believe that the way we live is simply "the way things should be." As a result, we often see our behavior as correct. However, culture is not value-neutral. We have good reasons for believing and behaving as we do, but that doesn't necessarily mean that others are "wrong."

Adopting the right attitude

You don't have to adopt the local culture and begin doing things the way they do. Just be aware and respect that they do things differently. "Your way" of communicating might work brilliantly in your own culture, but less well in another. Try to adopt an open-minded approach, focusing on:

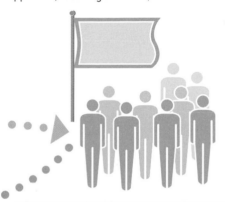

- **Developing a tolerance for ambiguity** Accept the fact that you'll never understand everything about another culture. However, you can still appreciate and function within that culture satisfactorily.
- **Becoming more flexible** Things won't always go the way you want. A small measure of flexibility will prove enormously helpful.
- **Practicing a little humility** Acknowledge what you do not know or understand. Because you weren't raised in another's culture (or may not even speak the language well), you'll never fully understand all aspects of it. Displaying humility and acceptance will win friends, influence people, and make life easier. Communication consists of the transfer of meaning, so do everything you can to make sure that your messages are not misunderstood.

ASK YOURSELF...
Do I understand the culture?

	YES	NO
1 Do I understand the **basic business etiquette** of introductions and meetings in this new culture?	☐	☐
2 Do I know how to recognize the **key decision-makers** within a group?	☐	☐
3 Am I familiar with the culture's **business dress code**?	☐	☐
4 Do I know how many **languages are spoken**, and which is the **official language**?	☐	☐
5 Have I learned the preferred **forms of negotiation**?	☐	☐
6 Do I know which **forms of media** are popular among which **demographic groups**?	☐	☐

Writing for the web

The way that people read a website is very different from the way in which they read other written information. You must take this into account when developing content for a website. It is not sufficient to simply repurpose content written for print; you need to write specifically for the internet, thinking carefully about your audience and what they need.

Engaging your readers

Why is writing for the internet different? First, people rarely read websites word for word. Instead, they scan the page, picking out individual words and sentences. Rather than starting at the beginning of a page and reading from start to finish, internet readers will scan a site looking for relevant items and then, if they find something useful, print it for later reference. Guide your reader by highlighting the most important or useful points in your document using headings, lists, and eye-catching typography.

Preparing content for the web

Try to provide information in **segments** or "chunks," and use **lists** rather than paragraphs—this will allow readers to quickly **find** what they're looking for

THINK ABOUT LENGTH

Limit the length of each **paragraph** and each **page** to about half of what you might consider for a printed page. Don't arbitrarily divide a page that is likely to be printed.

AVOID FRAGMENTATION

Be careful not to **subdivide** your information into too many pieces. Your readers may be overwhelmed or frustrated if they have too many choices. Ensure that each segment is **sensibly organized, coherent**, and **easy to scan**.

16%

of users read a web page **word for word**; most people only **scan** the text, picking out **highlighted words**, bold or colored **section headings**, and bulleted points

Navigation aids

Web readers generally do not read pages in sequence. Instead, they jump around on a website looking for content that interests them, navigating back and forth across images, ideas, and words. Providing information in precise segments or "chunks" will allow readers to quickly find what they're looking for. A well-constructed chunk provides readers with a comprehensive account, as well as links to related or supporting pages. When your content lends itself to such treatment, use lists rather than paragraphs. Readers can pick out information more easily from a list than from a fully developed paragraph.

ENSURE EASY ACCESS

Your principal goal should be to **provide access** to the information people are most likely to want. Provide **easy-to-follow clues** that will lead people to chunks of information that will be useful to them.

USE SUMMARIES

Include brief but **comprehensive summaries** of longer documents, so that readers can easily tell whether they need to read more or can move on to other content.

PREPARE FOR PRINT

Make it easy for your readers to find, print, and save information. If some aspects of your content are more detailed or lengthy, consider **linking to a PDF** file that is both downloadable and printable.

Communicating through social media

Social channels on the internet—notably Facebook, Twitter, Google Plus, and LinkedIn—have transformed the way people do business. A social media presence is no longer an option, but an essential—more than 80 percent of people are influenced in their buying decisions by a brand's presence on social media. So how do you maximize the impact of your social media output?

Devise a strategy

Social media can be used in many different ways—from increasing awareness of your company's brand, increasing traffic to your website, and forging new business contacts at home and abroad, to boosting sales or attracting customers to stores. So, the first decision you should make is to set the purpose of your social media interaction. Be specific in your goals, and list them in order of importance.

Next, carry out some research—formal or informal—into the internet habits of your customers or target audience: who are they? Which social media channels do they use? What do

they expect from these channels? You will have far more success if you tune in to the needs of your customers.

58%
of adult users of **social networks** follow at least one brand

Focus on success

Always consider how your social media activities will translate into business growth—there is little point in maintaining a costly presence on social channels if it doesn't affect the bottom line. Think about how you can measure the effectiveness of your activities. Having a large number of followers on Facebook or Twitter, for example, may be impressive, but may be of little value

Three major uses of social media

	SELLING	BUILDING PROFILE	CUSTOMER SERVICE
ACTIVITIES	O Posting information and user reviews of new products. O Announcing events or sales. O Issuing vouchers or discounts.	O Providing useful information or resources for users. O Becoming the "go to" place for discussion of an industry topic.	O Engaging with customer queries and solving their problems. O Measuring customers' sentiments toward your business.
REMEMBER TO	O Balance the hard sell with useful content and user interaction.	O Keep your content lively, current, and varied. Just giving links to other web sites will not encourage repeat visits from others.	O Set up a separate account for this purpose and ensure that your responses are quick and authoritative.

if it fails to translate into improved business performance. Similarly, building up many connections on LinkedIn may be of little use if you fail to leverage these connections to create new business. Always consider how you'll gauge the value of the effort you invest in social media.

Remember too what social media is—social. Too many companies use it as a one-way form of communication, like a corporate website, and fail to invite user comment or contribution. The more dialogue you can build with your customers, the more effective your use of social channels will be.

Engaging with your audience

How you communicate through social channels depends on your goals (see above). However, you should always:

- Post regularly: a media stream to which you contribute sporadically will soon dry up.
- Post interesting comments: try to encourage debate, comment, or likes, rather than making passive statements.
- Vary contributors for differing perspectives.
- Always respond to posts from users within a reasonable time frame.

Running a teleconference

Recent improvements in technology have made video conferencing an essential tool for many businesses. Whether you are using a dedicated teleconferencing system or a computer package such as Skype, it is vital to plan carefully to avoid technical hitches and make the experience rewarding and successful for those involved.

Preparing for a teleconference

Running a successful and productive teleconference depends largely on the time you spend planning and preparing for it. If possible, find out as much as you can about the facility you have chosen before the day of the teleconference. If you're in charge, it is up to you to make sure that the setting has everything you need. Try to meet with the support technician, if there is one, and learn what your physical responsibilities will involve.

Plan your teleconference

Visit the facility in advance and try to identify any aspects of the location or equipment that affect how you need to plan the teleconference.

Identify the purpose of the teleconference: explain to people what they will be doing and why.

Plan the agenda; don't just try to "wing it" as you go along. Place easily accomplished items first on the list.

Identify a chairperson who will be responsible for starting, stopping, and running the teleconference.

CHAIRING A TELECONFERENCE

Dos	Don'ts
O Asking people to give their names, titles, and locations	O Introducing some of the participants, but ignoring others
O Keeping to the agenda and staying on time	O Introducing new items not agreed to in advance
O Taking control and providing people with opportunities to speak	O Allowing people to talk with one another in side conversations
O Making notes of what is being said and by whom	O Failing to capture what's been said and agreed to

Success depends on the time you spend planning and **preparing for the teleconference**: try to find out as much as you can about **the facility** you have **chosen**

Share important resources in advance; send through any materials that are important for everyone to see.

Confirm the teleconference with all participants and send a reminder just before it is due to take place.

Distribute the agenda so other people know what will be discussed and will have time to gather necessary information.

Schedule the teleconference for a time and date that suits everyone.

Appearing well

On the day, dress conservatively: avoid busy patterns, thin stripes, and small prints that draw attention. Act always as if people are watching you, and refrain from quirky mannerisms—these may go unnoticed in a meeting but are magnified in a teleconference. Sit up straight, pay attention, and project a professional image. Make sure you know where the camera lens is before you start the call —it is not always above the screen. Make sure to look directly at the camera lens when you are speaking. You'll enhance your credibility dramatically if you focus squarely on the camera; others will think you're speaking directly to them.

Ensure the office from which you are calling is **neat** and that there's nothing distracting in the **background.**

Pay particular attention to the lighting in the room, making make sure that **your face is well lit**; try placing a large sheet of white paper flat on the desk in front of you to **reduce any harsh shadows** on your face.

Try moving your computer's video camera closer to you so that your **head and upper shoulders** occupy the whole screen—any smaller and it becomes difficult to see and read your facial expressions.

Succeeding with Skype

Larger companies often have dedicated video-conferencing systems housed in rooms that are optimized for the purpose —and a technician to maintain the facility. However, if you work for a smaller firm or from home, you will probably use a computer-based conferencing system such as Skype and so must take responsibility for all aspects of a call.

The more you use Skype, the easier and more natural it becomes, but be aware of a few simple tips that'll make your calls more professional and productive.

Add another light behind you to illuminate the room and provide a sense of place.

Use the **fastest internet connection** you have available.

Close other programs on your computer—especially if they make a noise (email clients, for example).

Check what the other person **can see** before you call.

Look into the camera, not at your picture on the screen.

Take some time to **get to know the program's controls**, so that you can—for example—mute the microphone if necessary.

Use gestures and expressions to **emphasize** your words

Sounding good

Once you're in the room, avoid idle talk or unguarded comments—assume that someone may be watching and listening. Speak a bit more slowly than usual, to ensure that everyone understands you, and use gestures and facial expressions to emphasize your words. Don't read a speech or a prepared statement, but keep summarizing key issues as you move along. Refer to the agenda and remind people of elapsed time as you move from point to point.

Switch off any potential distractions, such as the telephone, and set your Skype status to "**Do not disturb**" so that you won't get interrupted by other incoming calls.

At the end of the teleconference, summarize the issues discussed and agreed to. After the event, prepare and distribute minutes within a few days.

Communicating in a crisis

There is a huge difference between business problems and crises. Problems are commonplace in business. A crisis, on the other hand, is a major, unpredictable event. Without careful communication, crises have the potential to damage an organization's reputation and financial standing, together with those of its employees, shareholders, products, and services.

Identifying the crisis

Some business crises can be prepared for (to a certain extent), while others require an immediate and creative response. There are two main types:

● **Internal crises** These arise within the company, such as accounting scandals, or labor strikes.
● **External crises** These are caused by an external factor, such as a natural disaster, a technological disaster, or external threats by special-interest groups.

It is important to recognize the type of crisis you are facing, because this will help you pinpoint the groups of people you will need to communicate with, and give you an idea of how fast and how far the effects of the crisis could potentially spread.

> Assemble an effective **team** and isolate its members from other **day-to-day concerns**

CASE STUDY

MERCK & COMPANY

In September 2004, pharmaceutical firm Merck & Company made the decision to remove its painkilling drug Vioxx from the market because of cardiovascular risks. More than 100 million prescriptions had been written for the drug. Within 60 hours of the initial announcement, Merck's communications team launched a website and established a toll-free telephone number to address concerns. Traffic on the company's Vioxx website grew from 4,000 hits daily to 234,000 in just 24 hours. The toll-free number received more than 120,000 calls in the first six days following the announcement. Without its sophisticated web presence and competently staffed call center, Merck would not have been able to address the enormous wave of public concern that arose overnight about Vioxx, and its reputation would have been badly damaged.

Dealing with a crisis

Communicating in a crisis is different from managing a business problem. You are likely to be unprepared, have insufficient information, and be under time pressure. Crisis communication often offers few precedents to work from and intense scrutiny from outside the organization. This can lead to a loss of control and a sense of panic, so it is important to keep your head, and address the crisis systematically.

Addressing a crisis

WHAT TO DO	HOW TO DO IT
01 Get information	O Deal from an informed position and separate fact from rumor. Document what you know and don't know for sure. Become the source of reliable information, and keep the information flowing. O Determine the real problem in the short term and the long term. Check whether this is really your problem.
02 Put people in place	O Put someone in charge. Give him or her responsibility, authority, and the resources to get the job done. Tell people who it is. O Assemble an effective but nimble team. Staff it with the expertise needed, and provide resources. Isolate team members from other day-to-day concerns.
03 Draw up a plan	O Develop a strategy, which should include ways to resolve the problem, deal with affected parties, and communicate both today and in the long term. O Establish goals. Define your objectives for the short term, mid-term, and long term. Measure relentlessly and don't be discouraged by critics, negative press, or short-term failures.
04 Start communicating	O Centralize communications. Incoming communication provides intelligence, while outgoing communication gives a measure of control over what is being said about the situation. O Rely on a strictly limited number of spokespersons who are knowledgeable, authoritative, responsive, patient, and good humored.

Dealing with the media

Being the subject of a news media interview is never easy, and can be stressful and risky. You might say the wrong thing or forget to say what's most important about the subject of the interview, or your comments might be taken out context when they're aired. However, by following a few basic rules, you can limit risk and use the interview to your advantage.

Capitalizing on opportunity

Learn to see media interviews as an opportunity to reach a large audience. They represent a chance to tell your story and to inform the public of your business or expertise. They also offer an opportunity to address public concerns and set the record straight, if you're the subject of misinformation in the press.

They can be a forum in which to apologize if you've done something wrong, and a chance to reinforce the credibility of your organization and its leadership. Don't feel bullied into giving an interview if you're not ready: you can say "no" or delegate to another staff member who is more accustomed to dealing with the media.

Never feel bullied into **giving an interview** if you're not ready: you can say "no" or **delegate** the task

Preparing for an interview

The best way to **ensure a good interview** is thorough preparation.

Gather all the **information** you will need. Make sure you know the latest **facts and figures**.

Research the reporter; deal only with **established**, professional journalists.

CHECKLIST...
Succeeding in media interviews

	YES	NO
1 Are you clear about **what you hope to achieve** from the interview?	☐	☐
2 Do you know **which items of information** you can share, and which are confidential?	☐	☐
3 Have you decided on a method for **avoiding arguments** if the reporter goads you?	☐	☐
4 Do you know **how to respond** to false allegations, without repeating the phrases the reporter uses?	☐	☐
5 Are you focused on remaining **professional and likable**, no matter what happens in the interview?	☐	☐

Gather all the information you will need: make sure that you have the latest **facts and figures**

Tip

GET YOUR POINT IN EARLY
A reporter may not ask the one question you're most hoping to talk about. **Raise the issue** yourself, **get your points in**, and **repeat them frequently**. Use the free air time or print space to your benefit.

Ask your Public Affairs or Corporate Communication office for **help** and **guidance**.

Find out the **subject and background** of the story and ask who else is participating.

Double-check the **time**, **date**, and **location** of the interview.

Building brands

Communicating the essence of a brand is more than simply using words and visuals to convey an image. This is because a brand is both a process and a product. It's a living, breathing organism that must be nurtured and protected if it is to survive and thrive.

Winning hearts and minds

A brand is, first of all, a promise of an experience. It is what a product, service, or company stands for in the minds of customers and prospects. At its very core, a brand is a perception or a feeling. It's the feeling evoked when we think about a product or the company that delivers it. And, of course, a brand is the basis for differentiation in the marketplace—a way to separate yourself from all other competitors in the hearts and minds of your customers.

Defining the brand

The most crucial characteristics of a brand are content and consistency. To succeed, a brand must make a clear and unambiguous promise to its stakeholders (customers, employees, investors, suppliers, creditors, and others) and then deliver on that promise.

The Starbucks brand, for example, is clearly aligned with the customer experience. When regulars in Starbucks' coffee shops began to complain about the smell of hot breakfast sandwiches, the company's CEO Howard Schultz decided to focus on the core experience (and aromas) of freshly ground coffee, and the relaxing experience of visiting a Starbucks. Retail giant Wal-Mart's brand promise is "Everyday low prices." It makes no promises about customer service, brand-name products, or the shopping experience.

Communicating brand image

VISION

Be certain that one consistent, strategic **vision** drives your goals for the brand. Prioritize your plan to **deliver** on the promise (what is most important and why?). Align all stakeholders behind the vision.

CULTURE

Empower your entire organization to **get behind the brand**. Give them the authority, responsibility, resources, and training to **satisfy customer expectations**.

In focus

BRAND VALUE

Brands that have a clear sense of themselves and have worked diligently to deliver on their promises are often quite durable, withstanding economic downturns, changes in customer preferences, and game-changing innovations in their product category. The value of developing brands is highlighted in two quotes. John Stuart, former CEO of Quaker Oats Company, said: "If this company were split up, I would gladly give you the property, plant, and equipment, and I would take the brands and trademarks... and I would fare better than you." Carlton Curtis, VP of Corporate Communication at Coca-Cola, stated: "If all of Coca-Cola's assets were destroyed overnight, whoever owned the Coca-Cola name could walk into a bank the next morning and get a loan to rebuild everything."

ACTION

Specify and communicate those actions that are **essential to brand success** to those within the organization who must deliver on the promise.

VALUE

Consistently and continually **measure results**. Show your investors, associates, and business partners what you've accomplished and what improvements you have yet to make.

INNOVATION

You cannot stand still; you must **continually innovate** to stay ahead of the demands of the marketplace and the shifts in everything from demographics to target-group tastes and preferences. Demonstrate that you are both innovative and protective of the brand experience.

A **brand** helps separate you from your competitors in the **hearts and minds** of your customers

Index

Acknowledgments

Author's acknowledgments
My thanks to the good people at Cobalt id who have helped me condense decades of experience, teaching, and research into an interesting, readable volume. Had Marek Walisiewicz not called and asked me to consider this project, I'd never have gotten it done. My appreciation goes, in particular, to Kati Dye and the other talented artists, editors, and designers who've transformed my thoughts and observations into a lovely book. My thanks, as well, to Daniel Mills and the very professional staff of Dorling Kindersley whose diligence and professionalism with this title and this series have been nothing short of remarkable. Thanks to you all.

Dedication
To Pam, Colleen, Molly, and Kathleen. And to Jay, Cianan, and Ty. Your inspiration, patience, and support have been indispensable. Thank you for making this possible.

To my Notre Dame colleagues: Sandra, Cynthia, and Sondra. You are among the many who have encouraged me, corrected me, kept me honest, and held me accountable for my ideas. And to Andrea: teaching and writing are so much easier with your help.

And, of course, to my friends in the Management Communication Association and the Arthur W. Page Society. Thank you for the support, counsel, and good ideas. My life is richer for having shared your company.

Publisher's acknowledgments
The publisher would like to thank Hilary Bird for indexing, Judy Barratt for proofreading, and Charles Wills for coordinating Americanization.

Original edition:
Senior Editor Peter Jones
Senior Art Editor Helen Spencer
Executive Managing Editor Adèle Hayward
Managing Art Editor Kat Mead
Art Director Peter Luff
Publisher Stephanie Jackson
Production Editor Ben Marcus
Production Controller Hema Gohil
US Editor Margaret Parrish

First edition produced for Dorling Kindersley Limited by Cobalt id
www.cobaltid.co.uk